KU-634-568

INFLUENCE

SCIENCE AND PRACTICE

THE GRAPHIC EDITION

ROBERT B. CIALDINI

ILLUSTRATED BY NATHAN LUETH

First published in Great Britain in 2012 by
PROFILE BOOKS LTD
3A Exmouth House
Pine Street
London EC1R 0JH
www.profilebooks.com

First published in the United States of America in 2012 by
Round Table Companies
www.roundtablecompanies.com

Text copyright © Robert B. Cialdini, 2012
Illustration copyright © Writers of the Round Table Press, Round
Table Companies, 2012

10 9 8 7 6 5 4 3 2 1

Printed and bound in Great Britain by
Bell & Bain Ltd, Glasgow

The moral right of the author has been asserted.

All rights reserved. Without limiting the rights under copyright
reserved above, no part of this publication may be reproduced,
stored or introduced into a retrieval system, or transmitted, in
any form or by any means (electronic, mechanical, photocopying,
recording or otherwise), without the prior written permission of
both the copyright owner and the publisher of this book.

A CIP catalogue record for this book is available from the
British Library.

ISBN 978 1 84668 614 6

The paper this book is printed on is certified by the © 1996
Forest Stewardship Council A.C. (FSC). It is ancient-forest
friendly. The printer holds FSC chain of custody SGS-COC-2061

MIX
Paper from
responsible sources
FSC® C007785
FSC
www.fsc.org

INFLUENCE IS NARRATED BY ROBERT B. CIALDINI, WHO IS PORTRAYED AS A MILITARY COMMANDER AND STRATEGIST IN THE COMPLIANCE WAR--A NOT-SO-DISTANT FUTURE BATTLE BETWEEN DARK FORCES WHO SEEK TO TURN SOCIETY INTO MINDLESS DRONES, AND A LARGELY OBLIVIOUS GENERAL POPULATION THAT CIALDINI FIGHTS TO PROTECT. THE DARK FORCES EMPLOY "COMPLIANCE PROFESSIONALS" (BOTH HUMAN AND CYBERNETIC ROBOTS) AND MANUFACTURE WEAPONS OF MASS INFLUENCE IN THEIR QUEST TO TURN SOCIETY INTO AUTOMATONS

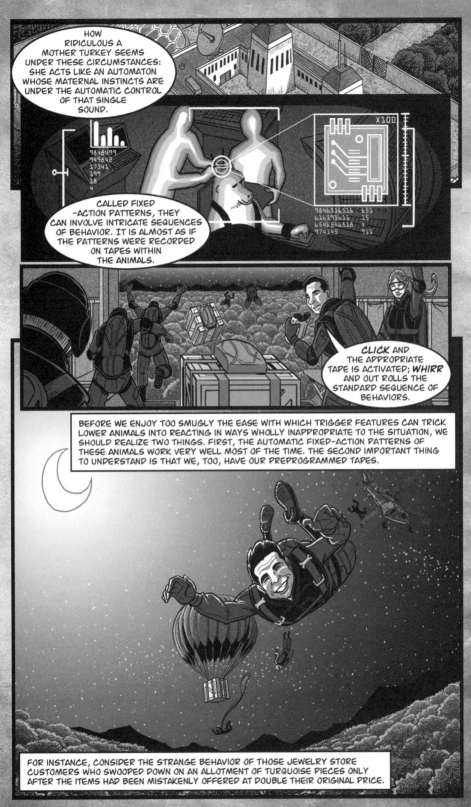

HOW RIDICULOUS A MOTHER TURKEY SEEMS UNDER THESE CIRCUMSTANCES: SHE ACTS LIKE AN AUTOMATON WHOSE MATERNAL INSTINCTS ARE UNDER THE AUTOMATIC CONTROL OF THAT SINGLE SOUND.

CALLED FIXED-ACTION PATTERNS, THEY CAN INVOLVE INTRICATE SEQUENCES OF BEHAVIOR. IT IS ALMOST AS IF THE PATTERNS WERE RECORDED ON TAPES WITHIN THE ANIMALS.

CLICK AND THE APPROPRIATE TAPE IS ACTIVATED; *WHIRR* AND OUT ROLLS THE STANDARD SEQUENCE OF BEHAVIORS.

BEFORE WE ENJOY TOO SMUGLY THE EASE WITH WHICH TRIGGER FEATURES CAN TRICK LOWER ANIMALS INTO REACTING IN WAYS WHOLLY INAPPROPRIATE TO THE SITUATION, WE SHOULD REALIZE TWO THINGS. FIRST, THE AUTOMATIC FIXED-ACTION PATTERNS OF THESE ANIMALS WORK VERY WELL MOST OF THE TIME. THE SECOND IMPORTANT THING TO UNDERSTAND IS THAT WE, TOO, HAVE OUR PREPROGRAMMED TAPES.

FOR INSTANCE, CONSIDER THE STRANGE BEHAVIOR OF THOSE JEWELRY STORE CUSTOMERS WHO SWOOPED DOWN ON AN ALLOTMENT OF TURQUOISE PIECES ONLY AFTER THE ITEMS HAD BEEN MISTAKENLY OFFERED AT DOUBLE THEIR ORIGINAL PRICE.

THESE WERE PEOPLE WHO HAD BEEN BROUGHT UP ON THE RULE, "YOU GET WHAT YOU PAY FOR" AND WHO HAD SEEN THAT RULE BORNE OUT OVER AND OVER IN THEIR LIVES. THE EXPENSIVE = GOOD STEREOTYPE HAD WORKED QUITE WELL FOR THEM IN THE PAST, SINCE NORMALLY THE PRICE OF AN ITEM INCREASES ALONG WITH ITS WORTH.

ALTHOUGH THEY PROBABLY DID NOT REALIZE IT, BY REACTING SOLELY TO THE PRICE OF THE TURQUOISE, THEY WERE PLAYING A SHORTCUT VERSION OF BETTING THE ODDS. THEY WERE BETTING THAT PRICE ALONE WOULD TELL THEM ALL THEY NEEDED TO KNOW.

AREA SECURE, SIR.

EXCELLENT. WE'LL SET UP BASE HERE FOR THE NIGHT AND WAIT FOR THE BRAVO TEAM.

YOU AND I EXIST IN AN EXTRAORDINARILY COMPLICATED ENVIRONMENT, EASILY THE MOST RAPIDLY MOVING AND COMPLEX THAT HAS EVER EXISTED ON THIS PLANET. TO DEAL WITH IT, WE **NEED** SHORTCUTS.

ABRAMS?

PSYCHOLOGISTS HAVE RECENTLY UNCOVERED A NUMBER OF MENTAL SHORTCUTS THAT WE EMPLOY IN MAKING OUR EVERYDAY JUDGEMENTS.*

TERMED *JUDGMENTAL HEURISTICS*, THESE SHORTCUTS OPERATE IN MUCH THE SAME FASHION AS THE EXPENSIVE = GOOD RULE, ALLOWING FOR SIMPLIFIED THINKING THAT WORKS WELL MOST OF THE TIME BUT LEAVES US OPEN TO OCCASIONAL, COSTLY MISTAKES.

THEY MAKE US TERRIBLY VULNERABLE TO ANYONE WHO DOES KNOW HOW THEY WORK.

*KAHNEMAN, SLOVIC, & TVERSKY, 1982; TODD & GIGERENZER, 2007.

TAKE, FOR EXAMPLE, THE DEADLY TRICK PLAYED BY THE KILLER FEMALES OF ONE GENUS OF FIREFLY (PHOTURIS) ON THE MALES OF ANOTHER FIREFLY GENUS (PHOTINUS).

WHAT DO FIREFLIES HAVE TO DO WITH—

POW biff smack

BY MIMICKING THE FLASHING MATING SIGNALS OF HER PREY, THE MURDERESS IS ABLE TO FEAST ON THE BODIES OF MALES WHOSE TRIGGERED COURTSHIP TAPES CAUSE THEM TO FLY MECHANICALLY INTO DEATH'S, NOT LOVE'S, EMBRACE.*

*LLOYD, 1965.

THERE ARE SOME PEOPLE WHO KNOW VERY WELL WHERE THE WEAPONS OF AUTOMATIC INFLUENCE LIE AND WHO EMPLOY THEM REGULARLY AND EXPERTLY TO GET WHAT THEY WANT.

A WOMAN EMPLOYING THE JAPANESE MARTIAL ART FORM CALLED JUJITSU WOULD USE HER OWN STRENGTH ONLY MINIMALLY AGAINST AN OPPONENT. INSTEAD, SHE WOULD EXPLOIT THE POWER INHERENT IN SUCH NATURALLY PRESENT PRINCIPLES AS GRAVITY, LEVERAGE, MOMENTUM, AND INERTIA.

AN EXAMPLE IS IN ORDER. THERE IS A PRINCIPLE OF HUMAN PERCEPTION, THE CONTRAST PRINCIPLE, THAT AFFECTS THE WAY WE SEE THE DIFFERENCE BETWEEN TWO THINGS THAT ARE PRESENTED ONE AFTER ANOTHER.

AUTOMOBILE DEALERS USE THE CONTRAST PRINCIPLE BY WAITING UNTIL THE PRICE OF A CAR HAS BEEN NEGOTIATED BEFORE SUGGESTING ONE OPTION AFTER ANOTHER. IN THE WAKE OF A MANY-THOU-SAND-DOLLAR DEAL, THE HUNDRED OR SO DOLLARS EXTRA FOR A NICETY LIKE AN UPGRADED CD PLAYER SEEMS ALMOST TRIVIAL IN COMPARISON.

THE PROFITEERS CAN COMMISSION THE POWER OF THESE WEAPONS FOR USE AGAINST THEIR TARGETS WHILE EXERTING LITTLE PERSONAL FORCE.

WE FOUND SOMETHING, SIR!

SEVERAL YEARS AGO, A UNIVERSITY PROFESSOR TRIED AN EXPERIMENT. HE SENT CHRISTMAS CARDS TO A SAMPLE OF PERFECT STRANGERS. THE GREAT MAJORITY OF THOSE WHO RETURNED CARDS NEVER INQUIRED INTO THE IDENTITY OF THE UNKNOWN PROFESSOR. THEY RECEIVED HIS HOLIDAY CARD, CLICK, AND WHIRR, THEY AUTOMATICALLY SENT CARDS IN RETURN.*

WHILE SMALL IN SCOPE, THIS STUDY SHOWS THE ACTION OF ONE OF THE MOST POTENT OF THE WEAPONS OF INFLUENCE AROUND US—THE RULE OF RECIPROCATION. THE RULE SAYS THAT WE SHOULD TRY TO REPAY, IN KIND, WHAT ANOTHER PERSON HAS PROVIDED US.

*KUNZ & WOOLCOTT, 1976.

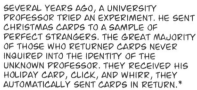

GET IT INSIDE.

TO UNDERSTAND HOW THE RULE OF RECIPROCATION CAN BE EXPLOITED BY ONE WHO RECOGNIZES IT AS THE WEAPON OF INFLUENCE IT CERTAINLY IS, WE MIGHT CLOSELY EXAMINE AN EXPERIMENT CONDUCTED BY PSYCHOLOGIST DENNIS REGAN (1971).

A SUBJECT WHO PARTICIPATED IN THE STUDY RATED, ALONG WITH ANOTHER SUBJECT, THE QUALITY OF SOME PAINTINGS AS PART OF AN EXPERIMENT ON "ART APPRECIATION."

DURING A SHORT REST PERIOD, "JOE" LEFT THE ROOM FOR A COUPLE OF MINUTES AND RETURNED WITH TWO BOTTLES OF COCA-COLA, ONE FOR THE SUBJECT AND ONE FOR HIMSELF; IN OTHER CASES, JOE RETURNED EMPTY-HANDED.

Joe "THE RATER"

Dr. REGAN, Dennis

LATER ON, AFTER THE PAINTINGS HAD ALL BEEN RATED AND THE EXPERIMENTER HAD MOMENTARILY LEFT THE ROOM, JOE ASKED THE SUBJECT TO DO HIM A FAVOR. HE INDICATED THAT HE WAS SELLING RAFFLE TICKETS, AND IF HE SOLD THE MOST TICKETS, HE WOULD WIN A $50 PRIZE.

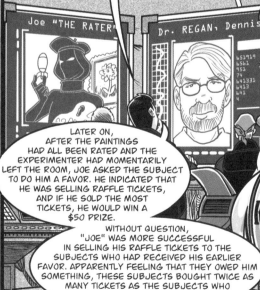

WITHOUT QUESTION, "JOE" WAS MORE SUCCESSFUL IN SELLING HIS RAFFLE TICKETS TO THE SUBJECTS WHO HAD RECEIVED HIS EARLIER FAVOR. APPARENTLY FEELING THAT THEY OWED HIM SOMETHING, THESE SUBJECTS BOUGHT TWICE AS MANY TICKETS AS THE SUBJECTS WHO HAD NOT BEEN GIVEN THE PRIOR FAVOR.

THERE'S ANOTHER WAY TO EMPLOY THE RECIPROCITY RULE TO GET SOMEONE TO COMPLY WITH A REQUEST.

I WAS WALKING DOWN THE STREET WHEN I WAS APPROACHED BY AN II- OR I2-YEAR-OLD BOY. HE INTRODUCED HIMSELF AND SAID HE WAS SELLING TICKETS TO THE ANNUAL BOY SCOUTS CIRCUS TO BE HELD ON THE UPCOMING SATURDAY NIGHT. HE ASKED IF I WISHED TO BUY ANY TICKETS AT $5 APIECE. I DECLINED.

"WELL," HE SAID, "IF YOU DON'T WANT TO BUY ANY TICKETS, HOW ABOUT BUYING SOME OF OUR CHOCOLATE BARS? THEY'RE ONLY $I EACH."

CLICK, WHIRR.

I BOUGHT A COUPLE AND, RIGHT AWAY, REALIZED THAT SOMETHING NOTEWORTHY HAD HAPPENED.

A) I DO NOT LIKE CHOCOLATE BARS.

B) I DO LIKE DOLLARS.

C) I WAS STANDING THERE WITH TWO OF HIS CHOCOLATE BARS.

D) HE WAS WALKING AWAY WITH TWO OF MY DOLLARS.

ANOTHER CONSEQUENCE OF THE RULE?

YES. AN OBLIGATION TO MAKE A CONCESSION TO SOMEONE WHO HAS MADE A CONCESSION TO YOU.

THE RECIPROCATION RULE BRINGS ABOUT MUTUAL CONCESSION IN TWO WAYS. THE FIRST IS OBVIOUS; IT PRESSURES THE RECIPIENT OF AN ALREADY-MADE CONCESSION TO RESPOND IN KIND. THE SECOND, WHILE NOT SO OBVIOUS, IS PIVOTALLY IMPORTANT.

BECAUSE OF A RECIPIENT'S OBLIGATION TO RECIPROCATE, PEOPLE ARE FREED TO MAKE THE INITIAL CONCESSION AND, THEREBY, TO BEGIN THE BENEFICIAL PROCESS OF EXCHANGE.

9

YOU WOULD THINK THAT THERE COULD BE A SUBSTANTIAL DISADVANTAGE TO THE TECHNIQUE AS WELL.

THE VICTIM MIGHT DECIDE NOT TO LIVE UP TO THE VERBAL AGREEMENT MADE WITH THE REQUESTER. OR THE VICTIM MIGHT COME TO DISTRUST THE MANIPULATIVE REQUESTER, DECIDING NEVER TO DEAL WITH THAT PERSON AGAIN.

RESEARCH INDICATES THAT THESE VICTIM REACTIONS DO NOT OCCUR WITH INCREASED FREQUENCY WHEN THE TECHNIQUE IS USED.

WHY WOULD THAT BE?

THE SECRET SIDE EFFECTS.

THE DESIRABLE SIDE EFFECTS OF MAKING CONCESSIONS DURING AN INTERACTION WITH OTHER PEOPLE ARE NICELY SHOWN IN STUDIES OF THE WAY PEOPLE BARTER WITH EACH OTHER.

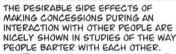

ONE EXPERIMENT, CONDUCTED BY SOCIAL PSYCHOLOGISTS AT UCLA, OFFERS AN ESPECIALLY APT DEMONSTRATION.*

*BENTON, KELLEY, & LIEBLING, 1972.

A SUBJECT IN THAT STUDY FACED A "NEGOTIATION OPPONENT" AND WAS TOLD TO BARGAIN WITH THE OPPONENT CONCERNING HOW TO DIVIDE BETWEEN THEMSELVES A CERTAIN AMOUNT OF MONEY PROVIDED BY THE EXPERIMENTERS. THE SUBJECT WAS ALSO INFORMED THAT IF NO MUTUAL AGREEMENT COULD BE REACHED AFTER A CERTAIN PERIOD OF BARGAINING, NO ONE WOULD GET ANY MONEY.

WITH SOME OF THE SUBJECTS, THE OPPONENT MADE AN EXTREME FIRST DEMAND AND STUBBORNLY PERSISTED IN THAT DEMAND THROUGHOUT THE NEGOTIATIONS.

WITH ANOTHER GROUP OF SUBJECTS, THE OPPONENT BEGAN WITH A DEMAND THAT WAS MODERATELY FAVORABLE TO HIMSELF; HE, TOO, STEADFASTLY REFUSED TO MOVE FROM THAT POSITION.

WITH A THIRD GROUP, THE OPPONENT BEGAN WITH THE EXTREME DEMAND AND THEN GRADUALLY RETREATED TO THE MORE MODERATE ONE DURING THE COURSE OF THE BARGAINING.

RESPONSIBILITY AND SATISFACTION!

SIR?

THE REQUESTER'S CONCESSION WITHIN THE REJECTION-THEN-RETREAT TECHNIQUE NOT ONLY CAUSED TARGETS TO SAY YES MORE OFTEN, IT ALSO CAUSED THEM TO FEEL MORE RESPONSIBLE FOR HAVING "DICTATED" THE FINAL AGREEMENT. AND SINCE THE TACTIC USES CONCESSION TO BRING ABOUT COMPLIANCE, THE VICTIM IS LIKELY TO FEEL MORE SATISFIED WITH THE AGREEMENT AS A RESULT. THE SECRET SIDE EFFECTS!

11

IF THAT WAS THEIR BEST ATTEMPT AT AN AMBUSH, THIS WILL BE A PIECE OF CAKE.

I WOULDN'T BE SO CERTAIN. NOW THEY'VE COMMITTED THEMSELVES TO THE FIGHT.

YOU MEAN THERE'LL BE MORE OF THESE THINGS?!

YOU DIDN'T THINK WE'D BRING A DESK JOCKEY LIKE YOU ALL THE WAY OUT HERE FOR JUST ONE WEAPON?

THERE WILL BE MORE. A STUDY DONE BY A PAIR OF CANADIAN PSYCHOLOGISTS* UNCOVERED SOMETHING FASCINATING ABOUT PEOPLE AT THE RACETRACK: JUST AFTER PLACING BETS THEY ARE MUCH MORE CONFIDENT OF THEIR HORSE'S CHANCE OF WINNING THAN THEY ARE IMMEDIATELY BEFORE LAYING DOWN THE BETS.

WE SIMPLY CONVINCE OURSELVES THAT WE HAVE MADE THE RIGHT CHOICE AND, NO DOUBT, FEEL BETTER ABOUT OUR DECISION.** IT IS, QUITE SIMPLY, OUR DESIRE TO BE—AND TO APPEAR—CONSISTENT WITH WHAT WE HAVE ALREADY DONE.

*KNOX & INKSTER, 1968.

**FAZIO, BLASCOVICH, & DRISCOLL, 1992.

TAKE, FOR EXAMPLE, MY NEIGHBOR SARA AND HER LIVE-IN BOYFRIEND, TIM.

SARA WANTED TIM TO MARRY HER AND TO STOP HIS HEAVY DRINKING; TIM RESISTED BOTH IDEAS. AFTER AN ESPECIALLY DIFFICULT PERIOD OF CONFLICT, SARA BROKE OFF THE RELATIONSHIP AND TIM MOVED OUT.

AT THE SAME TIME, AN OLD BOYFRIEND OF SARA'S CALLED HER. THEY STARTED SEEING EACH OTHER SOCIALLY AND QUICKLY BECAME ENGAGED AND MADE WEDDING PLANS. THEY HAD GONE SO FAR AS TO SET A DATE AND ISSUE INVITATIONS WHEN TIM CALLED. HE HAD REPENTED AND WANTED TO MOVE BACK IN. TIM EVEN OFFERED TO MARRY HER, BUT SHE STILL SAID SHE PREFERRED THE OTHER BOYFRIEND.

FINALLY, TIM VOLUNTEERED TO QUIT DRINKING IF SHE WOULD ONLY RELENT.

WITHIN A MONTH, TIM INFORMED SARA THAT HE DIDN'T THINK HE NEEDED TO STOP DRINKING AFTER ALL. A MONTH LATER, HE DECIDED THAT THEY SHOULD "WAIT AND SEE" BEFORE GETTING MARRIED. TWO YEARS HAVE SINCE PASSED.

SARA IS MORE DEVOTED TO HIM THAN SHE EVER WAS.

NO WORD FROM BRAVO TEAM YET?

NO, SIR.

PACK IT IN. THEY ALREADY KNOW WE'RE HERE, SO LEAVE THE TENTS AS DECOYS. WE'RE ON THE MOVE.

ABRAMS, DON'T FORGET: YOU ASKED TO COME ON THIS MISSION.

TO UNDERSTAND WHY CONSISTENCY IS SO POWERFUL A MOTIVE, WE SHOULD RECOGNIZE THAT, IN MOST CIRCUMSTANCES, CONSISTENCY IS VALUED AND ADAPTIVE. THE PERSON WHOSE BELIEFS, WORDS, AND DEEDS DON'T MATCH IS SEEN AS CONFUSED, TWO-FACED, EVEN MENTALLY ILL. A HIGH DEGREE OF CONSISTENCY IS NORMALLY ASSOCIATED WITH PERSONAL AND INTELLECTUAL STRENGTH.

WHEN IT OCCURS UNTHINKINGLY, CONSISTENCY CAN BE DISASTROUS. NONETHELESS, EVEN BLIND CONSISTENCY HAS ITS ATTRACTIONS.

ONCE WE HAVE MADE UP OUR MINDS ABOUT ISSUES, STUBBORN CONSISTENCY ALLOWS US A VERY APPEALING LUXURY: WE DON'T HAVE TO THINK HARD ABOUT THE ISSUES ANYMORE. ALL WE HAVE TO DO WHEN CONFRONTED WITH THE ISSUES IS CLICK ON OUR CONSISTENCY TAPE, WHIRR, AND WE KNOW JUST WHAT TO BELIEVE, SAY, OR DO.

THERE IS A SECOND, MORE PERVERSE ATTRACTION OF MECHANICAL CONSISTENCY AS WELL. THERE ARE CERTAIN DISTURBING THINGS WE SIMPLY WOULD RATHER NOT REALIZE. BECAUSE IT IS A PREPROGRAMMED AND MINDLESS METHOD OF RESPONDING, AUTOMATIC CONSISTENCY CAN SUPPLY A SAFE HIDING PLACE FROM TROUBLING REALIZATIONS.

ONCE WE REALIZE THAT THE POWER OF CONSISTENCY IS FORMIDABLE IN DIRECTING HUMAN ACTION, AN IMPORTANT PRACTICAL QUESTION IMMEDIATELY ARISES: HOW IS THAT FORCE ENGAGED?

SOCIAL PSYCHOLOGISTS THINK THEY KNOW THE ANSWER: COMMITMENT. IF I CAN GET YOU TO MAKE A COMMITMENT (THAT IS, TO TAKE A STAND, TO GO ON RECORD), I WILL HAVE SET THE STAGE FOR YOUR AUTOMATIC AND ILL-CONSIDERED CONSISTENCY WITH THAT EARLIER COMMITMENT.

DURING THE KOREAN WAR, MANY CAPTURED AMERICAN SOLDIERS FOUND THEMSELVES IN PRISONER-OF-WAR CAMPS RUN BY THE CHINESE COMMUNISTS. SPECIFICALLY AVOIDING THE APPEARANCE OF BRUTALITY, THE RED CHINESE ENGAGED IN WHAT THEY TERMED THEIR "LENIENT POLICY," WHICH WAS, IN REALITY, A CONCERTED AND SOPHISTICATED PSYCHOLOGICAL ASSAULT ON THEIR CAPTIVES.

THESE PRISONERS HAD BEEN TRAINED TO PROVIDE NOTHING BUT NAME, RANK, AND SERIAL NUMBER. THE CHINESE ANSWER WAS ELEMENTARY: START SMALL AND BUILD.

YOU SAID IT: THE UNITED STATES IS NOT PERFECT. YOU AGREED THAT IN A COMMUNIST COUNTRY, UNEMPLOYMENT IS NOT A PROBLEM.

NOW, JUST WRITE THIS ON THE PAPER.

LATER HE MIGHT BE ASKED TO READ HIS PAPER IN A DISCUSSION GROUP WITH OTHER PRISONERS.

THE CHINESE MIGHT THEN USE HIS NAME AND HIS PAPER IN AN ANTI-AMERICAN RADIO BROADCAST BEAMED NOT ONLY TO THE ENTIRE CAMP BUT TO OTHER POW CAMPS IN NORTH KOREA AS WELL AS TO AMERICAN FORCES IN SOUTH KOREA.

AWARE THAT HE HAD WRITTEN THE ESSAY WITHOUT ANY STRONG THREATS OR COERCION, MANY TIMES A MAN WOULD CHANGE HIS SELF-IMAGE TO BE CONSISTENT WITH THE DEED AND WITH THE NEW "COLLABORATOR" LABEL, OFTEN RESULTING IN EVEN MORE EXTENSIVE ACTS OF COLLABORATION.

THE TACTIC OF STARTING WITH A LITTLE REQUEST IN ORDER TO GAIN EVENTUAL COMPLIANCE WITH RELATED LARGER REQUESTS HAS A NAME: THE FOOT-IN-THE-DOOR TECHNIQUE.

THEY'VE GOT THE BRAVO TEAM.

EXAMINATION OF SUCH DIVERSE ACTIVITIES AS THE INDOCTRINATION PRACTICES OF THE CHINESE COMMUNISTS AND THE INITIATION RITUALS OF COLLEGE FRATERNITIES PROVIDES SOME VALUABLE INFORMATION ABOUT COMMITMENT.

NOTICE THAT ALL OF THE FOOT-IN-THE-DOOR EXPERTS SEEMS TO BE EXCITED ABOUT THE SAME THING: YOU CAN USE SMALL COMMITMENTS TO MANIPULATE A PERSON'S SELF-IMAGE. ONCE YOU'VE GOT A PERSON'S SELF-IMAGE WHERE YOU WANT IT, THAT PERSON SHOULD COMPLY **NATURALLY** WITH A WHOLE RANGE OF REQUESTS THAT ARE CONSISTENT WITH THIS NEW SELF-VIEW.

IT APPEARS THAT THE COMMITMENTS MOST EFFECTIVE IN CHANGING A PERSON'S SELF-IMAGE AND FUTURE BEHAVIOR ARE THOSE THAT ARE ACTIVE, PUBLIC, AND EFFORTFUL.

SOCIAL SCIENTISTS HAVE DETERMINED THAT **WE ACCEPT INNER RESPONSIBILITY FOR A BEHAVIOR WHEN WE THINK WE HAVE CHOSEN TO PERFORM IT IN THE ABSENCE OF STRONG OUTSIDE PRESSURE.**

A LARGE REWARD IS ONE SUCH EXTERNAL PRESSURE. THE SAME IS TRUE OF A STRONG THREAT; IT MAY MOTIVATE IMMEDIATE COMPLIANCE, BUT IT IS UNLIKELY TO PRODUCE LONG-TERM COMMITMENT.

AS SAMUEL BUTLER WROTE MORE THAN 300 YEARS AGO, "HE WHO AGREES AGAINST HIS WILL / IS OF THE SAME OPINION STILL."

THERE IS YET ANOTHER ATTRACTION IN COMMITMENTS THAT LEAD TO INNER CHANGE—THEY "GROW THEIR OWN LEGS."

THERE'S YOUR TARGET, ABRAMS. GO ON, I'LL COVER YOU.

BECAUSE WE BUILD NEW STRUTS TO UNDERGIRD CHOICES WE HAVE COMMITTED OURSELVES TO, AN EXPLOITATIVE INDIVIDUAL CAN OFFER US AN INDUCEMENT FOR MAKING SUCH A CHOICE. AFTER THE DECISION HAS BEEN MADE, THE INDIVIDUAL CAN REMOVE THAT INDUCEMENT, KNOWING THAT OUR DECISION WILL PROBABLY STAND ON ITS OWN NEWLY CREATED LEGS.

FOR CERTAIN CUSTOMERS, A VERY GOOD PRICE, PERHAPS AS MUCH AS $400 BELOW COMPETITORS' PRICES, IS OFFERED ON A CAR.

ONCE THE DECISION HAS BEEN MADE, A NUMBER OF ACTIVITIES DEVELOP THE CUSTOMER'S SENSE OF PERSONAL COMMITMENT TO THE CAR—A FISTFUL OF PURCHASE FORMS ARE FILLED OUT, EXTENSIVE FINANCING TERMS ARE ARRANGED, SOMETIMES THE CUSTOMER IS ENCOURAGED TO DRIVE THE CAR FOR A DAY BEFORE SIGNING THE CONTRACT.

CAR DEALERS FREQUENTLY TRY TO BENEFIT FROM THIS PROCESS THROUGH A TRICK THEY CALL "THROWING A LOW-BALL."

THEN SOMETHING HAPPENS.

OCCASIONALLY AN "ERROR" IN THE CALCULATIONS IS DISCOVERED—MAYBE THE SALESPERSON FORGOT TO ADD THE COST OF THE AIR CONDITIONER, AND IF THE BUYER STILL REQUIRES AIR CONDITIONING, $400 MUST BE ADDED TO THE PRICE.

THOSE WHO HAVE ONLY POOR CHOICES TO OFFER US ARE ESPECIALLY FOND OF THE TECHNIQUE.

LIKE MY NEIGHBOR, TIM.

SINCE HER DECISION TO CHOOSE TIM, SARA HAS BECOME MORE DEVOTED TO HIM THAN EVER, EVEN THOUGH HE HAS NOT FULFILLED HIS PROMISES. I KNOW FULL WELL THAT SARA IS A LOW-BALL VICTIM.

WE MUST BE WARY OF THE TENDENCY TO BE AUTOMATICALLY AND UNTHINKINGLY CONSISTENT, FOR IT LAYS US OPEN TO THE MANEUVERS OF THOSE WHO WANT TO EXPLOIT THE MECHANICAL COMMITMENT–CONSISTENCY SEQUENCE FOR PROFIT.

SO HOW DO WE BEAT THIS THING?

THERE ARE CERTAIN SIGNALS TO TIP US OFF. WE REGISTER EACH TYPE IN A DIFFERENT PART OF OUR BODIES.

THE FIRST OCCURS RIGHT IN THE PIT OF OUR STOMACHS WHEN WE REALIZE WE ARE TRAPPED INTO COMPLYING WITH A REQUEST WE *KNOW* WE DON'T WANT TO PERFORM. LET ME TELL YOU THIS STORY...

HELLO! I'M DOING A SURVEY OF ENTERTAINMENT HABITS OF CITY RESIDENTS, AND I WONDER IF YOU COULD ANSWER A FEW QUESTIONS FOR ME.

SURE.

HOW MANY TIMES PER WEEK DO YOU GO OUT TO DINNER?

THREE, MAYBE FOUR. I *LOVE* FINE RESTAURANTS.

DO YOU USUALLY ORDER WINE? DO YOU SEE MOVIES MUCH? CONCERTS? TOURING PERFORMANCES BY THEATRICAL OR BALLET COMPANIES?

WANTING TO MAKE A FAVORABLE IMPRESSION, I DO ADMIT, I STRETCHED THE TRUTH IN MY INTERVIEW ANSWERS IN ORDER TO PRESENT MYSELF IN THE MOST POSITIVE LIGHT.

I'M PLEASED TO SAY YOU COULD SAVE UP TO $1,200 A YEAR BY JOINING *CLUBAMERICA!* A SMALL MEMBERSHIP FEE...

I REMEMBER QUITE WELL FEELING MY STOMACH TIGHTEN AS I STAMMERED MY AGREEMENT. I HAD BEEN CORNERED BY MY OWN WORDS.

NO MORE, THOUGH. I LISTEN TO MY STOMACH THESE DAYS.

QUITE WRONG. NO *CLICK, WHIRR* FOR ME.

HUH?

LET ME PUT IT THIS WAY:

1) IT WOULD BE STUPID OF ME TO SPEND MONEY ON SOMETHING I DON'T WANT. 2) I HAVE IT ON EXCELLENT AUTHORITY, DIRECT FROM MY STOMACH, THAT I DON'T WANT YOUR ENTERTAINMENT PLAN. 3) IF YOU STILL BELIEVE I WILL BUY IT, YOU PROBABLY ALSO STILL BELIEVE IN THE TOOTH FAIRY.

WHAT IF YOUR STOMACH DOESN'T SAY ANYTHING?

STOMACHS ARE NOT ESPECIALLY PERCEPTIVE OR SUBTLE ORGANS. ONLY WHEN IT IS *OBVIOUS* THAT WE ARE ABOUT TO BE CONNED ARE THEY LIKELY TO REGISTER AND TRANSMIT THAT MESSAGE.

THE SITUATION OF MY NEIGHBOR SARA PROVIDES A GOOD ILLUSTRATION.

MY STOMACH SAYS NO!!!!

STOMACHS TELL US WHEN WE ARE DOING SOMETHING WE THINK IS WRONG FOR US. SARA *THINKS* NO SUCH THING.

YET, UNLESS I BADLY MISS MY GUESS, THERE IS A PART OF SARA THAT RECOGNIZES HER CHOICE AS A MISTAKE AND HER CURRENT LIVING ARRANGEMENT AS A BRAND OF FOOLISH CONSISTENCY.

WHERE, EXACTLY, THAT PART OF SARA IS LOCATED WE CAN'T BE SURE, BUT OUR LANGUAGE DOES GIVE IT A NAME: HEART OF HEARTS. IT IS, BY DEFINITION, THE ONE PLACE WHERE WE CANNOT FOOL OURSELVES.

PSYCHOLOGICAL EVIDENCE INDICATES THAT WE EXPERIENCE OUR FEELINGS TOWARD SOMETHING A SPLIT SECOND BEFORE WE CAN INTELLECTUALIZE ABOUT IT.* THEREFORE, IF WE TRAIN OURSELVES TO BE ATTENTIVE, WE SHOULD REGISTER THE FEELING EVER SO SLIGHTLY BEFORE OUR COGNITIVE APPARATUS ENGAGES.

*MURPHY & ZAJONC, 1993; VAN DEN BERG ET AL., 2006.

IN INDIVIDUALISTIC NATIONS SUCH AS THE UNITED STATES AND THOSE OF WESTERN EUROPE, THE FOCUS IS ON THE SELF, WHEREAS, IN MORE COLLECTIVISTIC SOCIETIES, THE FOCUS IS ON THE GROUP. FOR EXAMPLE, INDIVIDUALISTS DECIDE WHAT THEY SHOULD DO IN A SITUATION BY LOOKING PRIMARILY AT THEIR OWN HISTORIES, OPINIONS, AND CHOICES RATHER THAN THOSE OF THEIR PEERS.

POWER DOWN

PDEEEFFFOOOOoooooooo

CONNECTED
CONSISTENCY

COMMITMENT AND CONSISTENCY TACTICS ARE LIKELY TO WORK ESPECIALLY WELL ON MEMBERS OF INDIVIDUALISTIC SOCIETIES, PARTICULARLY THOSE WHO ARE OVER 50 YEARS OLD.

WHEN IT COMES TO ILLUSTRATING THE STRENGTH OF SOCIAL PROOF, THERE IS ONE ILLUSTRATION THAT IS FAR AND AWAY MY FAVORITE.

THE CULT OF THE GUARDIANS?

BINGO.

I'M NOT FAMILIAR WITH THE GUARDIANS, SIR.

DOOMSDAY CULT BASED IN CHICAGO. THEY WEREN'T THE FIRST AND WON'T BE THE LAST TO CLAIM THE WORLD IS ENDING, BUT FOLLOWING THE OBVIOUS FAILURE OF THE PROPHECIES, HISTORY RECORDS AN... ENIGMATIC PATTERN.

RATHER THAN DISBANDING IN DISILLUSION, THE CULTISTS OFTEN BECOME STRENGTHENED IN THEIR CONVICTIONS.

THE GUARDIANS WERE HEADED UP BY DR. THOMAS ARMSTRONG AND MRS. MARIAN KEECH. THE CULT OF BELIEVERS WAS SMALL, NEVER NUMBERING MORE THAN 30 MEMBERS.

KEECH, Marian AKA MARTIN, Dorothy

DR. ARMSTRONG, Thomas

THREE SOCIAL SCIENTISTS WHO WERE COLLEAGUES AT THE UNIVERSITY OF MINNESOTA HEARD ABOUT THE CULT AND DECIDED TO INVESTIGATE BY JOINING THE GROUP, INCOGNITO.

MRS. KEECH WAS THE CENTER OF ATTENTION AND ACTIVITY. EARLIER IN THE YEAR SHE HAD BEGUN TO RECEIVE MESSAGES FROM SPIRITUAL BEINGS, WHOM SHE CALLED THE GUARDIANS, LOCATED ON OTHER PLANETS.

21

THE TRANSMISSIONS FROM THE GUARDIANS GAINED NEW SIGNIFICANCE WHEN THEY BEGAN TO FORETELL OF A GREAT IMPENDING DISASTER— A FLOOD THAT WOULD BEGIN IN THE WESTERN HEMISPHERE AND EVENTUALLY ENGULF THE WORLD. BEFORE THE CALAMITY, SPACEMEN WERE TO ARRIVE AND CARRY OFF THE BELIEVERS IN FLYING SAUCERS TO A PLACE OF SAFETY.

AS THE SOCIAL SCIENTISTS, FESTINGER, RIECKEN, AND SCHACHTER OBSERVED THE PREPARATIONS DURING THE WEEKS PRIOR TO THE FLOOD DATE, THEY NOTED WITH SPECIAL INTEREST TWO SIGNIFI-CANT ASPECTS OF THE MEMBERS' BEHAVIOR.

FIRST, THE LEVEL OF COMMITMENT TO THE CULT'S BELIEF SYSTEM WAS VERY HIGH. MANY BELIEVERS QUIT THEIR JOBS OR NEGLECTED THEIR STUDIES.

THE SECOND SIGNIFICANT ASPECT WAS A CURIOUS FORM OF INACTION. THEY MADE NO ATTEMPT TO SEEK CONVERTS, TO PROSELYTE ACTIVELY.

AS THE TIME APPOINTED FOR THEIR DEPARTURE GREW VERY CLOSE, THE BELIEVERS SETTLED INTO A LULL OF SOUNDLESS ANTICIPATION.

4:45 A.M. 4.75 HOURS PAST ZERO HOUR.

MARIAN KEECH'S HAND SUDDENLY BEGAN TRANSCRIBING THROUGH "AUTOMATIC WRITING" THE TEXT OF A HOLY MESSAGE FROM ABOVE.

WITHIN MINUTES AFTER SHE HAD READ THE MESSAGE EXPLAINING THE DISCONFIRMATION, MRS. KEECH RECEIVED ANOTHER MESSAGE INSTRUCTING HER TO PUBLICIZE THE EXPLANATION.

This holy gathering has spread so much light that God has saved the world from destruction.

ALL CALLERS WERE ADMITTED, ALL QUESTIONS WERE ANSWERED, ATTEMPTS WERE MADE TO PROSELYTE ALL VISITORS.

ODDLY, IT WAS NOT THEIR PRIOR CERTAINTY THAT DROVE THE MEMBERS TO PROPAGATE THE FAITH, IT WAS AN ENCROACHING SENSE OF UNCERTAINTY.

I'VE TURNED MY BACK ON THE WORLD. I CAN'T AFFORD TO DOUBT. I HAVE TO BELIEVE. AND THERE ISN'T ANY OTHER TRUTH.*

SO MASSIVE WAS THE COMMIT-MENT TO THEIR BELIEFS THAT NO OTHER TRUTH WAS TOLERABLE.

*FESTINGER, ET AL., 1964, P. 168.

ANOTHER WAY THAT UNCERTAINTY DEVELOPS IS THROUGH LACK OF FAMILIARITY WITH A SITUATION.

CONSIDER HOW THIS SIMPLE INSIGHT ALLOWED ONE MAN TO BECOME A MULTIMILLIONAIRE.

HIS NAME WAS SYLVAN GOLDMAN AND, AFTER ACQUIRING SEVERAL SMALL GROCERY STORES IN 1934, HE NOTICED THAT HIS CUSTOMERS STOPPED BUYING WHEN THEIR HAND-HELD SHOPPING BASKETS GOT TOO HEAVY. THIS INSPIRED HIM TO INVENT THE SHOPPING CART.

THE CONTRAPTION WAS SO UNFAMILIAR-LOOKING THAT, AT FIRST, NONE OF GOLDMAN'S CUSTOMERS WAS WILLING TO USE IT.

HE BUILT AN ADEQUATE SUPPLY, PLACED THEM IN A PROMINENT PLACE, AND ERECTED SIGNS DESCRIBING THEIR BENEFITS, TO NO AVAIL.

FRUSTRATED AND ABOUT TO GIVE UP, HE TRIED ONE MORE IDEA TO REDUCE HIS CUSTOMERS' UNCERTAINTY—HE HIRED SHOPPERS TO WHEEL THE CARTS THROUGH THE STORE.

HE DIED A VERY RICH MAN.

ESPECIALLY IN AN AMBIGUOUS SITUATION, THE TENDENCY FOR EVERYONE TO BE LOOKING TO SEE WHAT EVERYONE ELSE IS DOING CAN LEAD TO A FASCINATING PHENOMENON CALLED **PLURALISTIC IGNORANCE.**

THE CLASSIC EXAMPLE OF SUCH BYSTANDER INACTION BEGAN AS AN ORDINARY HOMICIDE CASE IN NEW YORK CITY'S BOROUGH OF QUEENS. A WOMAN IN HER LATE TWENTIES WAS KILLED IN A LATE-NIGHT ATTACK ON HER STREET AS SHE RETURNED FROM WORK.

INCREDIBLY, 38 OF HER NEIGHBORS WATCHED FROM THE SAFETY OF THEIR APARTMENT WINDOWS WITHOUT SO MUCH AS LIFTING A FINGER TO CALL THE POLICE.

23

FORTUNATELY, OUR NEWFOUND UNDERSTANDING OF THE BYSTANDER "APATHY" PROCESS OFFERS REAL HOPE.

ONCE IT IS UNDERSTOOD THAT THE ENEMY IS THE SIMPLE STATE OF UNCERTAINTY, IT BECOMES POSSIBLE FOR EMERGENCY VICTIMS TO REDUCE THIS UNCERTAINTY, THEREBY PROTECTING THEMSELVES.

CLEARLY, THEN, AS A VICTIM, YOU MUST DO MORE THAN ALERT BYSTANDERS TO YOUR NEED FOR EMERGENCY ASSISTANCE; YOU MUST ALSO REMOVE THEIR UNCERTAINTIES ABOUT HOW THAT ASSISTANCE SHOULD BE PROVIDED AND WHO SHOULD PROVIDE IT. WHAT WOULD BE THE MOST EFFICIENT AND RELIABLE WAY TO DO SO?

YOU, SIR! IN THE BLUE JACKET! I NEED HELP. CALL AN AMBULANCE.

BOOP

WITHOUT QUESTION, WHEN PEOPLE ARE UNCERTAIN, THEY ARE MORE LIKELY TO USE OTHERS' ACTIONS TO DECIDE HOW THEY THEMSELVES SHOULD ACT. IN ADDITION, THERE IS ANOTHER IMPORTANT WORKING CONDITION: SIMILARITY.

THE PRINCIPLE OF SOCIAL PROOF OPERATES MOST POWERFULLY WHEN WE ARE OBSERVING THE BEHAVIOR OF PEOPLE JUST LIKE US.*

ONCE THE ENORMITY OF THAT FORCE IS RECOGNIZED, IT BECOMES POSSIBLE TO UNDERSTAND PERHAPS THE MOST SPECTACULAR ACT OF COMPLIANCE OF OUR TIME—THE MASS SUICIDE AT JONESTOWN, GUYANA.

*FESTINGER, 1954; PLATOW ET AL., 2005.

MEN, TODAY YOU WILL FACE THE SP WEAPON. ABRAMS HERE IS GOING TO GIVE YOU THE LOWDOWN ON THE DANGERS OF SOCIAL PROOF FROM THE MOST SPECTACULAR USE OF THE WEAPON IN OUR LIFETIMES.

THE PEOPLE'S TEMPLE WAS A CULT-LIKE ORGANIZATION THAT WAS BASED IN SAN FRANSISCO AND DREW ITS RECRUITS FROM THE POOR OF THAT CITY.

JIM JONES, THE GROUP'S UNDISPUTED POLITICAL, SOCIAL, AND SPIRITUAL LEADER, MOVED THE BULK OF THE MEMBERSHIP WITH HIM TO A JUNGLE SETTLEMENT IN GUYANA, SOUTH AMERICA.

THERE THE PEOPLE'S TEMPLE EXISTED IN RELATIVE OBSCURITY UNTIL NOVEMBER 18, 1978, WHEN CONGRESSMAN LEO R. RYAN OF CALIFORNIA, THREE MEMBERS OF RYAN'S FACT-FINDING PARTY, AND A CULT DEFECTOR WERE MURDERED AS THEY TRIED TO LEAVE JONESTOWN BY PLANE.

CONVINCED THAT HE WOULD BE ARRESTED AND IMPLICATED IN THE KILLINGS AND THAT THE DEMISE OF THE PEOPLE'S TEMPLE WOULD RESULT, JONES SOUGHT TO CONTROL THE END OF THE TEMPLE IN HIS OWN WAY.

HE GATHERED THE ENTIRE COMMUNITY AROUND HIM AND ISSUED A CALL FOR EACH PERSON'S DEATH TO BE DONE IN A UNIFIED ACT OF SELF-DESTRUCTION.

KEEP YOUR EYES AND EARS OPEN. DON'T LET THE SP'S SNEAK UP ON YOU.

BUT SIR, WHAT *CAUSED* THE GIANT ACT OF COMPLIANCE AT JONESTOWN?

ONE ESPECIALLY REVEALING QUESTION GIVES US A CLUE: "IF THE COMMUNITY HAD REMAINED IN SAN FRANCISCO, WOULD REVEREND JONES' SUICIDE COMMAND HAVE BEEN OBEYED?"

THIS WOULDN'T HAVE HAPPENED IN CALIFORNIA. BUT THEY LIVED IN TOTAL ALIENATION FROM THE REST OF THE WORLD IN A JUNGLE SITUATION IN A HOSTILE COUNTRY.

DR. LOUIS JOLYON WEST CHAIRMAN OF PSYCHIATRY AND BIOBEHAVIORAL SCIENCES, AUTHORITY ON CULTS.

IF WE ARE TO BELIEVE THE STORIES OF JIM JONES' MALEVOLENT GENIUS, HE REALIZED FULLY THE MASSIVE PSYCHOLOGICAL IMPACT SUCH A MOVE WOULD HAVE ON HIS FOLLOWERS.

IN THE ALIEN, GUYANESE ENVIRONMENT, THEN, TEMPLE MEMBERS WERE VERY READY TO FOLLOW THE LEAD OF OTHERS. AS WE HAVE ALSO SEEN, IT IS OTHERS OF A SPECIAL KIND WHOSE BEHAVIOR WILL MOST UNQUESTIONINGLY BE FOLLOWED: *SIMILAR* OTHERS.

THEREIN LIES THE AWFUL BEAUTY OF REVEREND JONES' RELOCATION STRATEGY. IN A COUNTRY LIKE GUYANA, THERE WERE NO SIMILAR OTHERS FOR A JONESTOWN RESIDENT BUT THE PEOPLE OF JONESTOWN ITSELF.

THERE A SETTLEMENT OF A THOUSAND PEOPLE, MUCH TOO LARGE TO BE HELD IN PERSISTENT SWAY BY THE FORCE OF ONE MAN'S PERSONALITY, COULD BE CHANGED FROM A FOLLOWING INTO A *HERD*.

SIMPLY GET SOME MEMBERS MOVING IN THE DESIRED DIRECTION AND THE OTHERS—RESPONDING NOT SO MUCH TO THE LEAD ANIMAL AS TO THOSE IMMEDIATELY SURROUNDING THEM—WILL PEACEFULLY AND MECHANICALLY GO ALONG.

THERE ARE TWO TYPES OF SITUATIONS IN WHICH INCORRECT DATA CAUSE THE PRINCIPLE OF SOCIAL PROOF TO GIVE US POOR COUNSEL. THE FIRST IS WHEN THE SOCIAL EVIDENCE HAS BEEN PURPOSELY FALSIFIED. THE CANNED LAUGHTER OF TV COMEDY SHOWS IS ONE VARIETY OF FAKED DATA OF THIS SORT.

THERE IS ANOTHER TIME WHEN THE PRINCIPLE OF SOCIAL PROOF WILL REGULARLY STEER US WRONG. IN SUCH AN INSTANCE, AN INNOCENT, NATURAL ERROR WILL PRODUCE SNOWBALLING SOCIAL PROOF THAT PUSHES US TO AN INCORRECT DECISION. THE PLURALISTIC IGNORANCE PHENOMENON, IN WHICH EVERYONE AT AN EMERGENCY SEES NO CAUSE FOR ALARM, IS ONE EXAMPLE OF THIS PROCESS.

FORTUNATELY, A QUICK GLANCE AROUND IS ALL THAT IS NEEDED. CERTAINLY, A FLIER FOLLOWING A LINE OF OTHERS WOULD BE WISE TO GLANCE OCCASIONALLY AT THE INSTRUMENT PANEL AND OUT THE WINDOW. IN THE SAME WAY, WE NEED TO LOOK UP AND AROUND PERIODICALLY WHENEVER WE ARE LOCKED INTO THE EVIDENCE OF THE CROWD.

WHAT'S GOING ON IN THERE, SIR?

INTEL SAYS THEY'RE COMBINING INFLUENCE WEAPONS.

FEW OF US WOULD BE SURPRISED TO LEARN THAT, AS A RULE, WE MOST PREFER TO SAY YES TO THE REQUESTS OF PEOPLE WE KNOW AND LIKE.

THE CLEAREST ILLUSTRATION I KNOW OF THE PROFESSIONAL EXPLOITATION OF THE LIKING RULE IS THE TUPPERWARE PARTY, WHICH I CONSIDER A CLASSIC COMPLIANCE SETTING. ANYBODY FAMILIAR WITH THE WORKINGS OF A TUPPERWARE PARTY WILL RECOGNIZE THE USE OF THE VARIOUS WEAPONS OF INFLUENCE WE HAVE EXAMINED SO FAR.

DESPITE THE ENTERTAINING AND PERSUASIVE SELLING SKILLS OF THE TUPPERWARE DEMONSTRATOR, THE TRUE REQUEST TO PURCHASE THE PRODUCT DOES NOT COME FROM THIS STRANGER; IT COMES FROM A FRIEND.

RECIPROCATION: PRIZES FOR ALL PARTYGOERS HANDED OUT.

COMMITMENT: PARTICIPANTS URGED TO PUBLICLY DESCRIBE USES AND BENEFITS THEY HAVE NOTICED.

SOCIAL PROOF: ONCE THE BUYING BEGINS, EACH PURCHASE BUILDS THE IDEA THAT OTHER, SIMILAR PEOPLE WANT THE PRODUCTS.

BY PROVIDING THE HOSTESS WITH A PERCENTAGE OF THE TAKE, THE TUPPERWARE HOME PARTIES CORPORATION ARRANGES FOR ITS CUSTOMERS TO BUY FROM AND FOR A FRIEND RATHER THAN FROM AN UNKNOWN SALESPERSON. THE RESULTS HAVE BEEN REMARKABLE.

COMPLIANCE PRACTITIONERS' WIDESPREAD USE OF THE LIKING BOND BETWEEN FRIENDS TELLS US MUCH ABOUT THE POWER OF THE LIKING RULE TO PRODUCE ASSENT. IN FACT, WE FIND THAT SUCH PROFESSIONALS SEEK TO BENEFIT FROM THE RULE EVEN WHEN ALREADY FORMED FRIENDSHIPS ARE NOT PRESENT FOR THEM TO EMPLOY.

WHO HAS THE CHARGES?

THERE IS A MAN IN DETROIT, JOE GIRARD, WHO SPECIALIZED IN USING THE LIKING RULE TO SELL CHEVROLETS. HE MADE HIS MONEY AS A SALESMAN ON THE SHOWROOM FLOOR. HE AVERAGED MORE THAN FIVE CARS AND TRUCKS EVERY DAY HE WORKED; AND HE HAS BEEN CALLED THE WORLDS "GREATEST CAR SALESMAN" BY THE *GUINNESS BOOK OF WORLD RECORDS*.

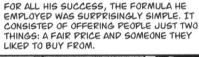

WORLD'S GREATEST SALESMAN

FOR ALL HIS SUCCESS, THE FORMULA HE EMPLOYED WAS SURPRISINGLY SIMPLE. IT CONSISTED OF OFFERING PEOPLE JUST TWO THINGS: A FAIR PRICE AND SOMEONE THEY LIKED TO BUY FROM.

ALTHOUGH IT IS GENERALLY ACKNOWLEDGED THAT GOOD-LOOKING PEOPLE HAVE AN ADVANTAGE IN SOCIAL INTERACTION, RECENT FINDINGS INDICATE THAT WE MAY HAVE SORELY UNDERESTIMATED THE SIZE AND REACH OF THAT ADVANTAGE.

THERE SEEMS TO BE A *CLICK, WHIRR* RESPONSE TO ATTRACTIVE PEOPLE.*

bKooM

*OLSON & MARSHUETZ, 2005.

29

FORTUNATELY, REAL HOPE FOR DRAINING AWAY THAT HOSTILITY IS EMERGING FROM THE RESEARCH OF EDUCATION SPECIALISTS INTO THE CONCEPT OF "COOPERATIVE LEARNING."

THE ESSENCE OF THE JIGSAW ROUTE TO LEARNING IS TO REQUIRE THAT STUDENTS WORK TOGETHER TO MASTER THE MATERIAL TO BE TESTED ON AN UPCOMING EXAMINATION. THIS END IS ACCOMPLISHED BY GROUPING STUDENTS INTO COOPERATING TEAMS AND GIVING EACH STUDENT ONLY PART OF THE INFORMATION—ONE PIECE OF THE PUZZLE—NECESSARY TO PASS THE TEST.

STUDIES HAVE SHOWN THAT, COMPARED TO OTHER CLASSROOMS IN THE SAME SCHOOL USING THE TRADITIONAL COMPETITIVE METHOD, JIGSAW LEARNING STIMULATED SIGNIFICANTLY MORE FRIENDSHIP AND LESS PREJUDICE AMONG ETHNIC GROUPS.

ANOTHER EXAMPLE OF LIKING IS THE GOOD COP/BAD COP ROUTINE.

IT'S BECAUSE OF NO-GOOD PUNKS LIKE YOU THAT—!

OKAY, FRANK, LET'S JUST CALM DOWN...

THE FEAR OF LONG INCARCERATION IS QUICKLY INSTILLED BY BAD COP'S THREATS; THE *PERCEPTUAL CONTRAST PRINCIPLE* ENSURES THAT COMPARED TO THE RAVING, VENOMOUS BAD COP, THE INTERROGATOR PLAYING GOOD COP WILL SEEM LIKE AN ESPECIALLY REASONABLE AND KIND PERSON*, AND BECAUSE GOOD COP HAS INTERVENED REPEATEDLY ON THE SUSPECT'S BEHALF, THE *RECIPROCITY RULE* PRESSURES FOR A RETURN FAVOR.**

THE MAIN REASON THAT THE TECHNIQUE IS EFFECTIVE, THOUGH, IS THAT IT GIVES THE SUSPECT THE IDEA THAT THERE IS SOMEONE ON HIS SIDE, SOMEONE WITH HIS WELFARE IN MIND, SOMEONE WORKING TOGETHER WITH HIM, FOR HIM.

*KASMISAR, 1980.
**RAFAELI & SUTTON, 1991.

BECAUSE LIKING CAN BE INCREASED BY MANY MEANS, A LIST OF THE DEFENSES AGAINST COMPLIANCE PROFESSIONALS WHO EMPLOY THE LIKING RULE MUST, ODDLY ENOUGH, BE A SHORT ONE.

THERE ARE SIMPLY TOO MANY ROUTES TO BE BLOCKED EFFECTIVELY WITH SUCH A ONE-ON-ONE STRATEGY.

BY CONCENTRATING OUR ATTENTION ON THE EFFECTS RATHER THAN THE CAUSES, WE CAN AVOID THE LABORIOUS, NEARLY IMPOSSIBLE TASK OF TRYING TO DETECT AND DEFLECT THE MANY PSYCHOLOGICAL INFLUENCES ON LIKING.

INSTEAD, WE HAVE TO BE SENSITIVE TO ONLY ONE THING RELATED TO LIKING IN OUR CONTACTS WITH COMPLIANCE PRACTITIONERS: THE FEELING THAT WE HAVE COME TO LIKE THE PRACTITIONER MORE QUICKLY OR MORE DEEPLY THAN WE WOULD HAVE EXPECTED.

ONCE WE NOTICE THIS FEELING, WE WILL HAVE BEEN TIPPED OFF THAT THERE IS PROBABLY SOME TACTIC BEING USED, AND WE CAN START TAKING THE NECESSARY COUNTERMEASURES. WE SHOULD STEP BACK FROM THE SOCIAL INTERACTION, MENTALLY SEPARATE THE REQUESTER FROM HIS OR HER OFFER, AND MAKE ANY COMPLIANCE DECISION BASED SOLELY ON THE MERITS OF THE OFFER.

TIME TO SPLIT UP. ABRAMS, CAPTAIN, WITH ME.

blam

ACCORDING TO THE BLUEPRINTS, THE HIGH SECURITY SECTORS SHOULD BE ON THE OTHER SIDE OF THIS ROOM.

WHAT'S THE AUTHORITY PROJECT?

SUPPOSE WHILE LEAFING THROUGH YOUR LOCAL NEWSPAPER, YOU NOTICE AN AD FOR VOLUNTEERS TO TAKE PART IN A "STUDY OF MEMORY" BEING DONE IN THE PSYCHOLOGY DEPARTMENT OF A NEARBY UNIVERSITY.

AUTHORITY PROJECT ▶

AH, HELLO! TODAY'S EXPERIMENT IS A STUDY OF HOW PUNISHMENT AFFECTS LEARNING AND MEMORY.

MR. JOHNSON HERE WILL BE THE "LEARNER," AND LEARN PAIRS OF WORDS IN A LONG LIST UNTIL EACH PAIR CAN BE RECALLED PERFECTLY.

YOU WILL BE THE "TEACHER" AND TEST THE LEARNER'S MEMORY AND DELIVER INCREASINGLY STRONG ELECTRIC SHOCKS FOR EVERY MISTAKE.

THERE WAS SUCH AN EXPERIMENT—ACTUALLY, A WHOLE SERIES—RUN BY A PSYCHOLOGY PROFESSOR NAMED MILGRAM, IN WHICH PARTICIPANTS IN THE TEACHER ROLE WERE WILLING TO DELIVER CONTINUED, INTENSE, AND DANGEROUS LEVELS OF SHOCK TO A KICKING, SCREECHING, PLEADING LEARNER.

ONLY ONE MAJOR ASPECT OF THE EXPERIMENT WAS NOT GENUINE. NO REAL SHOCK WAS DELIVERED; THE LEARNER, WHO REPEATEDLY CRIED OUT IN AGONY FOR MERCY AND RELEASE, WAS NOT A TRUE SUBJECT BUT AN ACTOR WHO ONLY PRETENDED TO BE SHOCKED.

65% OF THE SUBJECTS CARRIED OUT THEIR DUTIES FAITHFULLY THROUGH TO THE MAXIMUM SHOCK.

35

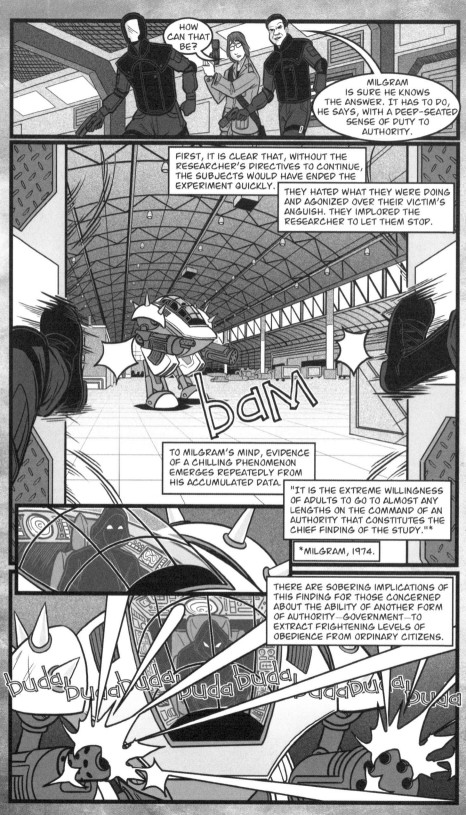

AFTER ALL, AS MILGRAM SUGGESTS, CONFORMING TO THE DICTATES OF AUTHORITY FIGURES HAS ALWAYS HAD GENUINE PRACTICAL ADVANTAGES FOR US. EARLY ON, THESE PEOPLE (PARENTS, TEACHERS) KNEW MORE THAN WE DID, AND WE FOUND THAT TAKING THEIR ADVICE PROVED BENEFICIAL.

AS ADULTS, THE SAME BENEFITS PERSIST FOR THE SAME REASONS, THOUGH THE AUTHORITY FIGURES ARE NOW EMPLOYERS, JUDGES, AND GOVERNMENT LEADERS.

THE PARADOX IS, OF COURSE, THE SAME ONE THAT ATTENDS ALL MAJOR WEAPONS OF INFLUENCE. IN THIS INSTANCE, ONCE WE REALIZE THAT OBEDIENCE TO AUTHORITY IS MOSTLY REWARDING, IT IS EASY TO ALLOW OURSELVES THE CONVENIENCE OF AUTOMATIC OBEDIENCE.

IT'S NO USE, IT'S JAMMED...

blam blam

EXAMPLE: MODERN MEDICINE. VARIOUS HEALTH WORKERS UNDERSTAND THE LEVEL OF THEIR JOBS IN THIS STRUCTURE, AND THEY WELL UNDERSTAND, TOO, THAT M.D.S SIT AT THE TOP. NO ONE MAY OVERRULE A DOCTOR'S JUDGMENT ON A CASE, EXCEPT, PERHAPS, ANOTHER DOCTOR OF HIGHER RANK.

I'M OUT OF AMMO, SIR!

THE WORRISOME POSSIBILITY ARISES, THEN, THAT WHEN A PHYSICIAN MAKES A CLEAR ERROR, NO ONE LOWER IN THE HIERARCHY WILL *THINK* TO QUESTION IT.

MIX THIS KIND OF *CLICK, WHIRR* RESPONSE INTO A COMPLEX HOSPITAL ENVIRONMENT AND MISTAKES ARE INEVITABLE.

WHEN IN A **CLICK**, **WHIRR** MODE, WE ARE OFTEN AS VULNERABLE TO THE SYMBOLS OF AUTHORITY AS TO THE SUBSTANCE. SEVERAL OF THESE SYMBOLS CAN RELIABLY TRIGGER OUR COMPLIANCE IN THE ABSENCE OF THE GENUINE SUBSTANCE OF AUTHORITY.

TITLES ARE SIMULTANEOUSLY THE MOST DIFFICULT AND THE EASIEST SYMBOLS OF AUTHORITY TO ACQUIRE. AS WE HAVE SEEN, ACTORS IN TV COMMERCIALS AND CON ARTISTS DO IT SUCCESSFULLY ALL THE TIME.

I'M NOT A DOCTOR, BUT I PLAY ONE ON TV.

A SECOND KIND OF AUTHORITY SYMBOL THAT CAN TRIGGER OUR MECHANICAL COMPLIANCE IS CLOTHING. POLICE BUNCO FILES BULGE WITH RECORDS OF CON ARTISTS WHOSE METHODS INCLUDE THE QUICK CHANGE. IN CHAMELEON STYLE, THEY ADOPT THE HOSPITAL WHITES, PRIESTLY BLACK, ARMY GREEN, OR POLICE BLUE THAT THE SITUATION REQUIRES FOR MAXIMUM ADVANTAGE.

TAKES MORE THAN A UNIFORM TO FOOL ME.

ASIDE FROM ITS FUNCTION IN UNIFORMS, CLOTHING CAN SYMBOLIZE A MORE GENERALIZED TYPE OF AUTHORITY WHEN IT SERVES AN ORNAMENTAL PURPOSE. FINELY STYLED AND EXPENSIVE CLOTHES CARRY AN AURA OF STATUS AND POSITION, AS DO SIMILAR TRAPPINGS SUCH AS JEWELRY AND CARS.

ACCORDING TO THE FINDINGS OF A STUDY DONE IN THE SAN FRANCISCO BAY AREA, OWNERS OF PRESTIGE AUTOS RECEIVE A SPECIAL KIND OF DEFERENCE FROM OTHERS. THE EXPERIMENTERS DISCOVERED THAT MOTORISTS WOULD WAIT SIGNIFICANTLY LONGER BEFORE HONKING THEIR HORNS AT A NEW, LUXURY CAR STOPPED IN FRONT OF A GREEN TRAFFIC LIGHT THAN AT AN OLDER, ECONOMY MODEL.*

THAT'S GREAT, SIR. BUT HOW ARE WE GOING TO BEAT THIS THING?!

DOOB & GROSS, 1968

THAT'S FIVE WEAPONS DOWN, SIR. WHAT'S LEFT?

EVER HEAR OF THE SCARCITY PRINCIPLE?

I DON'T BELIEVE SO, SIR.

WELL, THEN, LET ME TELL YOU A STORY. THE CITY OF MESA, ARIZONA, IS A SUBURB IN THE PHOENIX AREA WHERE I LIVE. PERHAPS THE MOST NOTABLE FEATURES OF MESA ARE ITS SIZABLE MORMON POPULATION AND A HUGE MORMON TEMPLE LOCATED ON EXQUISITELY KEPT GROUNDS IN THE CENTER OF THE CITY.

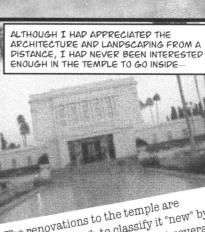

ALTHOUGH I HAD APPRECIATED THE ARCHITECTURE AND LANDSCAPING FROM A DISTANCE, I HAD NEVER BEEN INTERESTED ENOUGH IN THE TEMPLE TO GO INSIDE—

The renovations to the temple are extensive enough to classify it "new" by church standards. For the next several days only, non-Mormon visitors will be allowed.

—UNTIL THE DAY I READ A NEWSPAPER ARTICLE THAT TOLD OF A SPECIAL INNER SECTOR OF MORMON TEMPLES TO WHICH NO ONE HAS ACCESS BUT FAITHFUL MEMBERS OF THE CHURCH.

I IMMEDIATELY RESOLVED TO TAKE A TOUR; BUT WHEN I PHONED A FRIEND TO ASK IF HE WANTED TO COME ALONG, I CAME TO UNDERSTAND SOMETHING THAT CHANGED MY DECISION JUST AS QUICKLY.

IT BECAME CLEAR AS I SPOKE THAT THE SPECIAL LURE OF THE TEMPLE HAD A SOLE CAUSE: IF I DID NOT EXPERIENCE THE RESTRICTED SECTOR SOON, I WOULD NEVER AGAIN HAVE THE CHANCE.

THE EVIDENCE, THEN, IS CLEAR. COMPLIANCE PRACTITIONERS' RELIANCE ON SCARCITY AS A WEAPON OF INFLUENCE IS FREQUENT, WIDE-RANGING, SYSTEMATIC, AND DIVERSE.

WITH THE SCARCITY PRINCIPLE, THE POWER COMES FROM TWO MAJOR SOURCES. THE FIRST IS FAMILIAR. LIKE THE OTHER WEAPONS OF INFLUENCE, THE SCARCITY PRINCIPLE TRADES ON OUR WEAKNESS FOR SHORTCUTS.

WE KNOW THAT THE THINGS THAT ARE DIFFICULT TO GET ARE TYPICALLY BETTER THAN THOSE THAT ARE EASY TO GET.*

IN ADDITION, THERE IS A UNIQUE, SECONDARY SOURCE OF POWER—

—AS OPPORTUNITIES BECOME LESS AVAILABLE, WE LOSE FREEDOMS. THE DESIRE TO PRESERVE OUR ESTABLISHED PREROGATIVES IS THE CENTERPIECE OF THE **PSYCHOLOGICAL REACTANCE** THEORY, DEVELOPED BY PSYCHOLOGIST JACK BREHM. ACCORDING TO THE THEORY, WHENEVER FREE CHOICE IS LIMITED OR THREATENED, THE NEED TO RETAIN OUR FREEDOMS MAKES US WANT THEM SIGNIFICANTLY MORE THAN BEFORE.

*LYNN, 1989.

TWO-YEAR-OLDS SEEM MASTERS OF THE ART OF RESISTANCE TO OUTSIDE PRESSURE, ESPECIALLY FROM THEIR PARENTS. TELL THEM ONE THING, THEY DO THE OPPOSITE; GIVE THEM ONE TOY, THEY WANT ANOTHER; PICK THEM UP AGAINST THEIR WILL, THEY WRIGGLE AND SQUIRM TO BE PUT DOWN; PUT THEM DOWN AGAINST THEIR WILL, THEY CLAW AND STRUGGLE TO BE CARRIED.

BY TESTING SEVERELY THE LIMITS OF THEIR FREEDOMS, THE CHILDREN ARE DISCOVERING WHERE IN THEIR WORLDS THEY CAN EXPECT TO BE CONTROLLED AND WHERE TO BE IN CONTROL.

GOT SOMETHING, SIR!

COOKIES

I DIDN'T DO THAT! THE DOOR IS OPENING ON ITS OWN!

PERHAPS, IN FINE JUJITSU STYLE, WE CAN USE THE AROUSAL ITSELF AS OUR PRIME CUE. IN THIS WAY, WE CAN TURN THE ENEMY'S STRENGTH TO OUR ADVANTAGE.

BY LEARNING TO FLAG THE EXPERIENCE OF HEIGHTENING AROUSAL IN A COMPLIANCE SITUATION, WE CAN ALERT OURSELVES TO THE POSSIBILITY OF SCARCITY TACTICS THERE AND TO THE NEED FOR CAUTION.

SHUNK

SIX WEAPONS NEUTRALIZED, SIR. MISSION OBJECTIVE ONE, COMPLETE.

OBJECTIVE ONE?! YOU MEAN THERE'S ANOTHER ONE???

NEUTRALIZE THE ENEMY AT THE SOURCE. WE'RE HEADING FOR BUNKER 2.

BACK IN THE 1960'S A MAN NAMED JOE PYNE HOSTED A RATHER REMARKABLE TV TALK SHOW THAT WAS SYNDICATED FROM CALIFORNIA. THE HOST'S ABRASIVE APPROACH WAS DESIGNED TO PROVOKE HIS GUESTS INTO ARGUMENTS, TO FLUSTER THEM INTO EMBARRASSING ADMISSIONS, AND GENERALLY TO MAKE THEM LOOK FOOLISH.

I GUESS YOUR LONG HAIR MAKES YOU A GIRL.

I GUESS YOUR WOODEN LEG MAKES YOU A TABLE.

THIS IS A CLASSIC ILLUSTRATION. VERY OFTEN WHEN WE MAKE A DECISION ABOUT SOMEONE OR SOMETHING WE DON'T USE ALL OF THE RELEVANT AVAILABLE INFORMATION.

ABRAMS, CALL UP THOSE BLUEPRINTS. GET US OUT OF HERE.

46

RECALL THAT EARLIER, WE COMPARED THIS SHORTCUT TO THE AUTOMATIC RESPONDING OF LOWER ANIMALS, WHOSE ELABORATE BEHAVIOR PATTERNS COULD BE TRIGGERED BY THE PRESENCE OF A LONE STIMULUS FEATURE—A CHEEP-CHEEP SOUND.

THE REASON THESE LOWER ANIMALS MUST OFTEN RELY ON SUCH SOLITARY STIMULUS FEATURES OF THEIR ENVIRONMENTS IS THEIR RESTRICTED MENTAL CAPACITY.

WE, OF COURSE, HAVE VASTLY MORE EFFECTIVE BRAIN MECHANISMS THAN DO MOTHER TURKEYS.

STILL, WE HAVE OUR CAPACITY LIMITATIONS, TOO; AND, FOR THE SAKE OF EFFICIENCY, WE MUST SOMETIMES RETREAT FROM THE TIME-CONSUMING, SOPHISTICATED, FULLY INFORMED BRAND OF DECISION MAKING TO A MORE AUTOMATIC, PRIMITIVE, SINGLE-FEATURE TYPE OF RESPONDING.

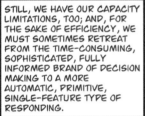

WE ARE LIKELY TO USE THESE LONE CUES WHEN WE DON'T HAVE THE INCLINATION, TIME, ENERGY, OR COGNITIVE RESOURCES TO UNDERTAKE A COMPLETE ANALYSIS OF THE SITUATION.

WE'VE GOT A WAY OUT, SIR. CHOPPER'S ON THE WAY.

WITH THE SOPHISTICATED MENTAL APPARATUS WE HAVE USED TO BUILD WORLD EMINENCE AS A SPECIES, WE HAVE CREATED AN ENVIRONMENT SO COMPLEX, FAST-PACED, AND INFORMATION-LADEN THAT WE MUST INCREASINGLY DEAL WITH IT IN THE FASHION OF THE ANIMALS WE LONG AGO TRANSCENDED.

ACCORDING TO YEARLY GALLUP POLLS, THE ISSUES RATED AS MOST IMPORTANT ON THE PUBLIC AGENDA ARE BECOMING MORE DIVERSE AND ARE SURVIVING ON THAT AGENDA FOR A SHORTER TIME.

IN ADDITION, WE TRAVEL MORE AND FASTER; WE RELOCATE MORE FREQUENTLY TO NEW RESIDENCES, WHICH ARE BUILT AND TORN DOWN MORE QUICKLY; WE CONTACT MORE PEOPLE AND HAVE SHORTER RELATIONSHIPS WITH THEM; IN THE SUPERMARKET, CAR SHOWROOM, AND SHOPPING MALL, WE ARE FACED WITH AN ARRAY OF CHOICES AMONG STYLES AND PRODUCTS THAT WERE UNHEARD OF LAST YEAR AND MAY WELL BE OBSOLETE OR FORGOTTEN BY NEXT YEAR.

THIS AVALANCHE OF INFORMATION AND CHOICES IS MADE POSSIBLE BY BURGEONING TECHNOLOGICAL PROGRESS. WITH FURTHER DEVELOPMENTS IN TELECOMMUNICATIONS AND TECHNOLOGY, ACCESS TO SUCH STAGGERING AMOUNTS OF INFORMATION IS FALLING WITHIN THE REACH OF INDIVIDUAL CITIZENS.

OUR MODERN ERA, OFTEN TERMED THE INFORMATION AGE, HAS NEVER BEEN CALLED THE KNOWLEDGE AGE. INFORMATION DOES NOT TRANSLATE DIRECTLY INTO KNOWLEDGE.

BECAUSE TECHNOLOGY CAN EVOLVE MUCH FASTER THAN WE CAN, OUR NATURAL CAPACITY TO PROCESS INFORMATION IS LIKELY TO BE INCREASINGLY INADEQUATE TO HANDLE THE ABUNDANCE OF CHANGE, CHOICE, AND CHALLENGE THAT IS CHARACTERISTIC OF MODERN LIFE.

MORE AND MORE FREQUENTLY, WE WILL FIND OURSELVES IN THE POSITION OF LOWER ANIMALS—WITH A MENTAL APPARATUS THAT IS UNEQUIPPED TO DEAL THOROUGHLY WITH THE INTRICACY AND RICHNESS OF THE OUTSIDE ENVIRONMENT.

WHEN THOSE SINGLE FEATURES ARE TRULY RELIABLE, THERE IS NOTHING INHERENTLY WRONG WITH THE SHORTCUT APPROACH OF NARROWED ATTENTION AND AUTOMATIC RESPONDING TO A PARTICULAR PIECE OF INFORMATION.

THE PROBLEM COMES WHEN SOMETHING CAUSES THE NORMALLY TRUSTWORTHY CUES TO COUNSEL US POORLY, TO LEAD US TO ERRONEOUS ACTIONS AND WRONGHEADED DECISIONS.

SIR, WHAT CAN WE DO ABOUT THE EXPECTED INTENSIFIED ATTACK ON OUR SYSTEM OF SHORTCUTS?

FORCEFUL COUNTERATTACK.

COMPLIANCE PROFESSIONALS WHO PLAY FAIRLY BY THE RULES OF SHORTCUT RESPONDING ARE NOT TO BE CONSIDERED THE ENEMY. THE PROPER TARGETS FOR COUNTER-AGGRESSION ARE ONLY THOSE INDIVIDUALS WHO FALSIFY, COUNTERFEIT, OR MISREPRESENT THE EVIDENCE THAT NATURALLY CUES OUR SHORTCUT RESPONSES.

WE SHOULD REFUSE TO WATCH TV PROGRAMS THAT USE CANNED LAUGHTER. IF WE SEE A BARTENDER BEGIN A SHIFT BY SALTING THE TIP JAR WITH A BILL OR TWO, THAT BARTENDER SHOULD GET NO TIP FROM US. IF, AFTER WAITING IN LINE OUTSIDE A NIGHTCLUB, WE DISCOVER FROM THE AMOUNT OF AVAILABLE SPACE THAT THE WAIT WAS DESIGNED TO IMPRESS PASSERSBY WITH FALSE EVIDENCE OF THE CLUB'S POPULARITY, WE SHOULD LEAVE IMMEDIATELY AND ANNOUNCE OUR REASON TO THOSE STILL IN LINE.

49

THE SIX
PRINCIPLES
OF INFLUENCE

AUTHORITY

CONSISTENCY

RECIPROCATION

SOCIAL PROOF

SCARCITY

LIKING

DR. ROBERT B. CIALDINI, AUTHOR

Dr. Robert Cialdini has spent his entire career researching the science of influence, earning him an international reputation as an expert in the fields of persuasion, compliance, and negotiation.

His books, including *Influence: Science & Practice*, are the results of years of study into the reasons why people comply with requests in business settings. Worldwide, *Influence* has sold over 2 million copies. *Influence* has been published in twenty-five languages.

His most recent co-authored book, *Yes! 50 Scientifically Proven Ways to be Persuasive*, has been on the *New York Times*, *USA Today*, and *Wall Street Journal* Best Seller Lists.

In the field of influence and persuasion, Dr. Cialdini is the most cited living social psychologist in the world today.

Dr. Cialdini received his Ph.D from the University of North Carolina and post doctoral training from Columbia University. He has held Visiting Scholar Appointments at Ohio State University, the University of California, the Annenberg School of Communications, and the Graduate School of Business of Stanford University. Currently, Dr. Cialdini is Regents' Professor Emeritus of Psychology and Marketing at Arizona State University.

Dr. Cialdini is President of INFLUENCE AT WORK, an international consulting, strategic planning and training organization based on the Six Principles of Influence.

NADJA BAER, STORY ADAPTATION

Nadja has been a words-nerd all her life. She speaks English, German, Italian, and Spanish (with varying degrees of fluency), can teach Taekwondo classes in Korean, and is currently working on expanding her French vocabulary. Since receiving a Bachelor's degree in Creative Writing at the University of Minnesota, she has served as the office thesaurus, dictionary, translator, and spell-checker in every one of her day jobs. She wrote her first terrible novella at the age of eight, and is now focused on writing comics and novels for young adults. Her work can be seen for free in the online graphic novel, *Impure Blood* (www.impurebloodwebcomic.com), which is drawn by her soon-to-be husband. Other projects she has scripted for Round Table include *Everything's Okay* (Sept 2011) and *Delivering Happiness* (March 2012). Aside from a love of a good story with pretty pictures, they share a house, a cat, a turtle, and a belief that more people should embrace their inner nerd.

NATHAN LUETH, ILLUSTRATION

Nathan Lueth came into existence with a pencil in his hand, a feat that continues to confound obstetricians to this day. No one knows for sure when he started drawing or where his love of comics came from, but most experts agree that his professional career began after graduating from the Minneapolis College of Art and Design, as a caricaturist in the Mall of America. Soon he was freelance illustrating for the likes of Target, General Mills, and Stone Arch Books.

When not drawing comics for other people, Nathan draws his own super awesome fantasy webcomic, *Impure Blood* (www.impurebloodwebcomic.com). He is proud to be a part of Writers of the Round Table, as he believes that comics should be for everyone, not just nerds (it should be noted that he may be trying to turn the general population into nerds). With Round Table he has illustrated *Overachievement* by Dr. John Eliot (April 2011) and a colored adaptation of *The U.S. Constitution* (March 2012). He resides in St. Paul, Minnesota, with a cat, a turtle, and his imminent wife, Nadja, upon whom he performs his nerd conversion experiments.